Diabetes

By Judith Peacock

Perspectives on Disease and Illness

LifeMatters
an imprint of Capstone Press
Mankato, Minnesota

LifeMatters Books are published by Capstone Press
818 North Willow Street • Mankato, Minnesota 56001
http://www.capstone-press.com

Printed in the United States of America

Library of Congress Cataloging-in-Publication Data
Peacock, Judith, 1942–
    Diabetes/by Judith Peacock.
      p. cm. — (Perspectives on disease and illness)
    Includes bibliographical references and index.
    Summary: Discusses the nature, types, symptoms, diagnosis,
    treatment, control, and complications of diabetes.
    ISBN 0-7368-0277-0 (book). — ISBN 0-7368-0294-0 (series)
    1. Diabetes Juvenile literature. [1. Diabetes. 2. Diseases.]
    I. Title. II. Series.
    RC660.5.P43 2000
    616.4´62—dc21   99-23879
                      CIP

Staff Credits
Kristin Thoennes, editor; Adam Lazar, designer; Kimberly Danger, photo researcher

Photo Credits
Cover: PNI/©Digital Vision, bottom, left, right; PNI/©Rubberball, middle
©Digital Visions/Family Healthcare, 13; Essential Foods, 30
International Stock/©Bill Stanton, 35, 39; ©John Michael, 24
©Leslie O'Shaughnessy, 7, 40, 43, 49
Photophile/©Tom Tracy, 57
Photri Inc./ 31
Rainbow/©Tom McCarthy, 15
Transparencies/©Tom McCarthy, 47, 53; ©J. Faircloth, 58
Unicorn Stock Photos/©Karen Holsinger Mullen, 17; ©Eric R. Berndt, 9; ©Jeff Greenberg, 20, 22

Table
of Contents

Chapter Overview

Diabetes is a serious disease. It has no cure and lasts a lifetime. It is not contagious like a cold or the flu.

In diabetes, the body does not use glucose properly. The body's cells need glucose for energy. High levels of glucose remain in the blood. A lack of insulin causes this problem.

People have known about diabetes since ancient times.

Diabetes today affects millions of people in North America.

Chapter 1

What Is Diabetes?

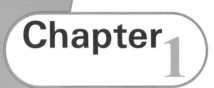

Molly felt angry and scared. Yesterday her **Molly, Age 16** doctor told her that she has diabetes. The doctor said she would have it for the rest of her life. "Why me?" cried Molly. "I'm only 16 years old!"

Molly was understandably upset. Diabetes is a serious, lifelong disease. It can lead to heart attack, kidney failure, blindness, and even death. There is no cure, but there is hope. People with diabetes can learn to manage their illness. They can live long and healthy lives.

The medical name for diabetes is *diabetes mellitus.* Doctors in ancient Greece and Rome named the disease. *Diabetes* means "passing through" in Greek. *Mellitus* means "sweet" or "honeyed" in Latin. The urine of people with diabetes contains sugar. It passes through the body quickly.

Too Much Sugar in the Blood

Diabetes affects the way the body uses food. The healthy body turns carbohydrates such as bread, rice, and potatoes into glucose. The body needs glucose, or blood sugar, for energy. The bloodstream delivers glucose to body cells. Then the glucose waits for the pancreas to do its job.

The pancreas is a small organ behind the stomach. It contains glands called the islets of Langerhans. These glands are made up of special cells. Beta cells are one type of cell in the islets of Langerhans. After a person eats, glucose floods the bloodstream. The beta cells quickly produce a hormone called insulin. Hormones are chemicals produced by the body. The insulin allows glucose to pass into the body's cells.

In diabetes, the body makes glucose as usual. The glucose enters the bloodstream, but then something goes wrong. In some people, the pancreas makes too little insulin or none at all. In others, the pancreas makes insulin, but the body doesn't use it well. Either way, the glucose cannot get into the body's cells. It builds up in the blood. Eventually it passes out of the body in urine.

An Ancient Disease

Diabetes has been around for thousands of years. An Egyptian manuscript from 1500 B.C. mentions a disease that caused people to urinate frequently. This is the oldest description of diabetes on record. A doctor in India in 400 B.C. described people who urinated as much as elephants. He noticed that flies liked the sweet-tasting urine of these people. Doctors in ancient Asia described symptoms such as thirst, tiredness, and skin boils.

Doctors in ancient times did not know the cause of diabetes. They did think it had something to do with diet. Around 100 A.D., a Greek doctor named Aretaeus of Cappadocia studied the symptoms of the disease. He prescribed a diet of milk, cereal, and wine. He wrote about the short life span of people with diabetes.

A 14-year-old boy was the first human to try insulin. Leonard Thompson weighed 75 pounds and was nearly dead. Then Frederick Banting and Charles Best injected him with insulin. The insulin shots lowered Leonard's blood sugar. He was able to eat and gained weight quickly.

Until the mid-1900s, children and teens with diabetes almost always died. In 1921, two Canadians, Frederick Banting and Charles Best, discovered insulin. They later found ways for human beings to use insulin from animals. In the 1950s, English scientist Frederick Sanger figured out the chemical structure of insulin. His work led to the manufacture of human insulin. These findings have helped people with diabetes live longer.

Diabetes Today

The cause of diabetes remains a mystery. The disease affects millions of North Americans. In the United States, 10.3 million people have been diagnosed with diabetes. Another 5.4 million have the disease but do not yet know it. Diabetes is the seventh-leading cause of death in the United States. In Canada, 1.5 million people have been diagnosed with diabetes. Another 750,000 have the disease but do not yet know it.

Frank read the facts and figures about diabetes. They were more than numbers to him. They meant a real person. Frank's mother was diagnosed with diabetes at the age of nine. She died at age 36. Frank's dad often says, "People with diabetes today have a better chance. The ways of treating diabetes are so much better. Your mom's organs just wore out from all that sugar."

Frank, Age 15

Experts say that one in five people has a chance of having diabetes. Everyone needs to know more about this disease.

Points to Consider

How much do you know about diabetes?

Does anyone in your family have diabetes? What is the disease like for them?

Do you know anyone in your school with diabetes?

How would you treat a classmate who has diabetes?

Chapter Overview

There are two main forms of diabetes. Type 1 occurs most often in children, teens, and young adults. Type 2 occurs most often in middle-aged adults who are overweight.

The symptoms of diabetes are frequent urination and excessive thirst and hunger. Other symptoms of type 1 are sudden weight loss and fatigue. Other symptoms of type 2 include numbness in the hands and feet and itchy skin. Some people with type 2 have no symptoms at all.

People with type 1 have little or no insulin. They depend on insulin shots to live. People with type 2 have insulin, but their body does not use it well. Usually they do not need insulin shots.

Millions of people have type 2 diabetes and do not yet know it.

Chapter 2

Types of Diabetes

Diabetes is not just one disease. Instead, diabetes includes several diseases. The two most common forms are type 1 and type 2. About 90 to 95 percent of people with diabetes have type 2. About 5 to 10 percent have type 1.

Teens have a greater chance of having type 1 diabetes than any other serious, chronic childhood disease.

Symptoms of Type 1 Diabetes

Chris squirmed in his chair. He had to go again! This was the fourth time since he got to school two hours ago. He felt stupid asking Ms. Potts for another lavatory pass.

Chris, Age 17

On his way back to class, Chris stopped at the drinking fountain. He took long gulps of water. Lately he seemed thirsty all the time. And hungry, too! Even though he had had a big breakfast, Chris was starving. "What's wrong with me?" he wondered.

Chris needs to see a doctor right away. He shows symptoms of type 1 diabetes. He goes to the bathroom a lot. He's very thirsty, and he's very hungry. Chris has lost 10 pounds in the last few weeks without trying. He feels tired and weak. People with type 1 may also have an upset stomach.

Symptoms of type 1 diabetes come on suddenly. Sometimes the symptoms look like the flu, strep throat, or an eating disorder. Type 1 diabetes can be dangerous. A person could go into a coma and die before the diabetes is discovered.

What Happens to the Body With Type 1?

In type 1 diabetes, the pancreas produces little or no insulin. Type 1 is called insulin-dependent diabetes. People with this form of the disease depend on daily insulin shots. They need these shots to live. People with type 1 diabetes also must eat a healthy diet and exercise often.

The body's immune system usually plays a role in type 1 diabetes. The immune system makes antibodies to fight viruses and bacteria. Sometimes these germ fighters make a mistake. They attack and kill the beta cells that produce insulin. Viruses that cause illnesses like the mumps or German measles also may trigger diabetes.

Teens who have type 2 diabetes are almost always overweight.

Type 1 diabetes used to be called juvenile-onset diabetes. It seemed to occur only in children, teens, and young adults. Now doctors know that type 1 can occur at any age. It affects both males and females. More whites have type 1 than any other race. Type 1 is the most severe form of diabetes.

Symptoms of Type 2 Diabetes

Lisa's dad is 46 years old and overweight. She teases him about being a couch potato. Mr. Shane complains that his hands and feet tingle. He itches all over. The same sore has been on his arm for several months. Lisa notices that her dad runs to the bathroom a lot.

Lisa, Age 14

Like Chris, Mr. Shane should see a doctor soon. He has symptoms of type 2 diabetes. Type 2 has some of the same symptoms as type 1. These include frequent urination and excessive hunger and thirst. In addition, people with type 2 diabetes may have numbness in their hands and feet. They also may itch all over their body. Their vision might be blurry. They may have skin infections that are hard to heal.

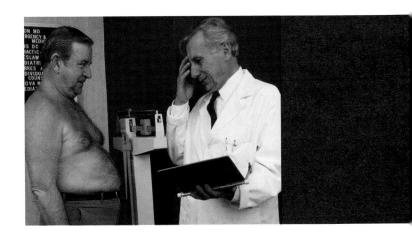

Some people with type 2 diabetes have no symptoms at all. In other people, the symptoms appear gradually. People may not even realize they have the disease. They wait to go to the doctor. By then, they may have serious problems with their eyes. Their nerves, kidneys, and heart also are in danger.

Type 2 diabetes used to be called adult-onset diabetes. It seemed to occur only in people over age 40. Now doctors know that type 2 diabetes also can develop in young people. Type 2 diabetes affects more females than males. Hispanics/Latinos, African Americans, American Indians, Asian Americans, and Pacific Islanders are in a higher risk category. People with type 2 often have a family history of diabetes.

What Happens to the Body With Type 2?

In type 2 diabetes, the body does not use insulin well. Being overweight can trigger this form of diabetes. Too much fat makes it difficult for insulin to do its job. Overeating strains the beta cells so they must struggle to produce insulin. Three-fourths of the people with type 2 diabetes are overweight.

Type 2 diabetes also is called noninsulin-dependent diabetes. People with type 2 usually do not need daily insulin shots. They can control their disease by eating healthy foods. They also must exercise and keep their weight down. Sometimes losing 10 to 20 pounds is enough to lower blood glucose levels.

People with type 2 diabetes might take pills if diet and exercise don't work. Diabetes pills help the body make better use of insulin. Sometimes people with type 2 must use insulin shots if the pills cannot control blood sugar.

Other Types of Diabetes

There are other forms of diabetes. Gestational diabetes may develop in pregnant women. This diabetes usually disappears after the baby is born. Impaired glucose tolerance is another type. People with this condition are at risk of having diabetes. Their blood glucose level falls between normal and diabetic.

Points to Consider

Do you know anyone who has the symptoms of diabetes? What kinds of symptoms do they have?

What would you do if you had symptoms of type 1 or type 2 diabetes?

What could you do to educate others about diabetes?

Chapter Overview

Doctors use blood tests to diagnose diabetes. They look at the level of sugar in the blood. Glucose levels that are above a certain point indicate diabetes.

People at risk for diabetes should have regular screening tests.

People with diabetic symptoms should have diagnostic tests. One kind of diagnostic test is the fasting blood glucose test. Another is the oral glucose tolerance test.

Doctors test the urine for ketones. Ketones are a sign of type 1 diabetes.

Chapter 3

Diagnosing Diabetes

Doctors use blood tests to diagnose diabetes. These tests measure the amount of glucose in the blood. Glucose levels that are too high mean diabetes.

Understanding Blood Sugar Levels

In a person without diabetes, the level of sugar in the blood rises and falls. It rises right after eating. Then it falls gradually. Insulin helps the glucose pass out of the blood. Exercise also lowers blood sugar levels.

The amount of sugar in the blood is measured in milligrams per deciliter (mg/dL). Normal fasting glucose should be less than 110 mg/dL. This is the level after not eating for 10 to 16 hours. Before meals, the normal range is between 70 and 120 mg/dL. Two hours after eating, the blood glucose level should be less than 180 mg/dL.

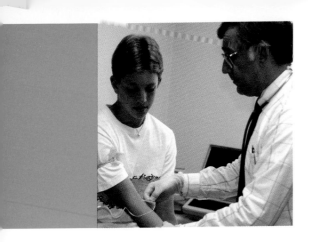

Screening Tests

Sam went to the doctor for a checkup. He needed his doctor's okay to play football.
The nurse drew blood from Sam's arm. The blood was tested for diabetes. Sam's blood glucose level was normal.

Sam, Age 17

Sam had a screening test for diabetes. Screening tests are simple and quick. Doctors use screening tests when there are no signs of diabetes. The test may be part of a routine checkup.

People at risk for diabetes should have regular screening tests. People at risk:

Have a parent or grandparent with diabetes

Have a brother or sister with diabetes

Are overweight

Are over age 40 and get little or no exercise

Are pregnant

Are African American, Hispanic/Latino, American Indian, Asian American, or Pacific Islander

Diagnostic Tests

Doctors use diagnostic tests to tell whether a person has diabetes. These tests are used when a person has diabetic symptoms. The tests also are used when a screening shows high blood sugar.

The Fasting Blood Glucose Test

The fasting blood glucose test is one diagnostic test. The person goes without eating overnight. The next morning, a nurse draws blood from a vein. Then the lab tests the blood sample. A blood sugar level of 126 mg/dL or higher may mean diabetes. The test must be repeated on another day. A doctor diagnoses diabetes if the reading is again 126 mg/dL or higher.

Give the risk test to your parents and other adults.

Take The Test. Know The Score.

Sixteen million Americans have diabetes—and one-third don't even know it! Take this test to see if you are at risk for having diabetes. Diabetes is more common in African Americans, Hispanics/Latinos, American Indians, Asian Americans, and Pacific Islanders. If you are a member of one of these ethnic groups, you need to pay special attention to this test.

To find out if you are at risk, write in the points next to each statement that is true for you. If a statement is not true put a zero. Add your total score.

1	My weight is equal to or above that listed in the chart.	**Yes 5**	____
2	I am 65 years of age *and* I get little or no exercise.	**Yes 5**	____
3	I am between 45 and 64 years of age.	**Yes 5**	____
4	I am 65 years or older.	**Yes 9**	____
5	I am a woman who has had a baby weighing more than nine pounds at birth.	**Yes 1**	____
6	I have a sister or a brother with diabetes.	**Yes 1**	____
7	I have a parent with diabetes.	**Yes 1**	____
		TOTAL	____

Scoring 3–9 Points

You are probably at low risk for having diabetes now. But don't just forget about it—especially if you are African American, Hispanic/Latino, American Indian, Asian American, or Pacific Islander. You may be at higher risk in the future. *New guidelines recommend everyone age 45 and over consider being tested for the disease every three years. However, people at high risk should consider being tested at a younger age.*

Scoring 10 or More Points

You are at high risk for having diabetes. Only your health care provider can determine if you have diabetes. See your health care provider soon and find out for sure.

At-Risk Weight Chart

If you weigh the same or more than the amount listed for your height, you may be at risk for diabetes. This chart is based on a measure called the Body Mass Index (BMI). The chart shows unhealthy weights for men and women age 35 or older at the listed heights. At-risk weights are lower for individuals under age 35.

Height*	Weight**	Height*	Weight**	Height*	Weight**
4' 10"	129	5' 4"	157	5' 10"	188
4' 11"	133	5' 5"	162	5' 11"	193
5' 0"	138	5' 6"	167	6' 0"	199
5' 1"	143	5' 7"	172	6' 1"	204
5' 2"	147	5' 8"	177	6' 2"	210
5' 3"	152	5' 9"	182	6' 3"	216
				6' 4"	221

*feet/inches without shoes
**pounds without clothing

Reprinted with permission from the American Diabetes Association, 1999.

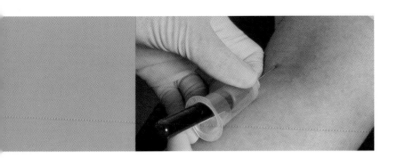

The Oral Glucose Tolerance Test

The oral glucose tolerance test is another diagnostic test. The test isn't painful, but it takes a long time.

Pam, Age 13

Pam arrived at the doctor's office early in the morning. She was starving. She hadn't eaten anything since dinner the night before.

The nurse took a sample of Pam's blood. The sample showed Pam's blood sugar level at the start of the test. Then Pam had to drink a can of sugary liquid. It tasted awful!

Every 30 minutes, the nurse stuck a needle in Pam's arm. This went on for two hours. Each blood sample was tested for glucose. The final sample was taken three hours after the test started. By this time, Pam felt like a pincushion.

The amount of glucose in Pam's blood rose after she drank the liquid. Instead of dropping, her blood sugar levels stayed high. After three hours, Pam's blood sugar level was 192 mg/dL. Her pancreas failed to make enough insulin. More tests proved that Pam had diabetes.

Type 1 or Type 2?

Doctors can tell the difference between type 1 and type 2 diabetes. They look at the blood tests. They consider the person's age, weight, and symptoms. Doctors might also test the person's urine for ketones. Ketones are poisonous wastes. They build up when the body burns fat for fuel instead of sugar. Ketones are a sign of type 1 diabetes.

Pam Learns More

After the diagnosis, Pam and her mother took classes to learn about diabetes. They learned how to give insulin shots. They learned about diet and exercise for people with diabetes. They went to the drugstore and bought the supplies that Pam would need. Pam began to realize the changes diabetes would make in her life.

Points to Consider

Have you had a screening test for diabetes? What was the result?

Are you at risk for diabetes? What should you do if you are at risk?

How would you feel if someone in your family were diagnosed with diabetes?

How would you convince someone to get a blood test for diabetes?

The goal of diabetes treatment is to control blood sugar levels. Insulin shots, a healthy diet, and exercise all can help lower blood sugar. All three must be part of a treatment plan for people with type 1 diabetes.

Controlling blood sugar levels is a constant job. People with diabetes must work at it every day of their life.

Doctors disagree on the best way to treat diabetes. Some use standard treatment. Most prefer tight control.

Many people can help teens manage their diabetes. Doctors, dietitians, parents, teachers, and coaches all can help.

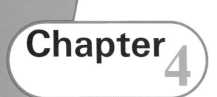

Chapter 4

Controlling Diabetes

Diabetes treatment has one goal. That goal is to keep blood sugar as close to a normal range as possible. People with diabetes must work at this goal constantly. Treatment for diabetes controls the disease. It does not cure the disease.

Each person with diabetes is different. Not everyone takes the same amount and type of insulin. The schedule for taking insulin also may vary. A doctor helps determine insulin needs.

Insulin Injections

> Between classes, Mark ducked into the nurse's office. The nurse handed him a needle and syringe. Mark pulled up his shirt. He stuck the needle in his belly and pressed down on the plunger.
>
> **Mark, Age 17**

Mark gave himself an insulin shot. People with type 1 diabetes, like Mark, must have daily insulin shots. Mark gives himself shots before meals. That way the insulin is ready when he needs it. Mark takes insulin at other times if his blood sugar is too high.

People with diabetes inject themselves all over their body. They inject insulin into their thighs, buttocks, belly, or upper arms. Insulin must be injected. It cannot be swallowed in pill form because insulin is a protein. The juices that digest food would destroy the insulin.

How Insulin Is Injected

There are different ways to inject insulin. Mark uses a needle and syringe. He fills the syringe with insulin from a small bottle. Some people use an insulin pen. It has a needle and an insulin cartridge. A jet injector has no needle. It shoots insulin directly into the skin. An insulin pump places a needle under the skin. It automatically delivers small doses of insulin all day long.

There are two sources of insulin. Animal insulin comes from the pancreas of cows or pigs. Human insulin is made in a laboratory.

There also are different speeds of insulin. Some insulins act quickly but for a short period. Long-acting insulin takes more time to reach the bloodstream. Its effects last longer. Some people take a short-acting insulin before eating. Then they may take a long-acting insulin in the morning and before bed. Some people may combine different speeds in one injection.

Blood Testing

Study hall was nearly over. Beth took a little needle out of a case. She pricked her finger. Beth let a drop of blood fall on a special chemical strip. Then she put the strip in a small device. After a few moments, a number appeared in the display window.

Beth, Age 16

After each test, Beth writes down the number, date, and time. She also writes what she was doing and how she felt. Beth shows her records to her doctor. Together they decide if Beth needs to change her treatment plan.

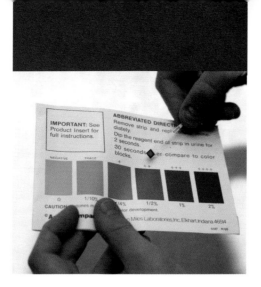

Beth checked her blood glucose level. She used a special needle called a lancet and a glucose meter. People with type 1 diabetes, like Beth, must test their blood two to four times each day. People with type 2 also should test their blood. They might do it once a day or once a week.

Self-testing blood sugar is an important part of controlling diabetes. It tells how well the treatment plan is working. It tells if insulin and food are in balance.

Urine Testing

People with type 1 diabetes should test their urine for ketones at certain times. They should test when their blood sugar is high. They also should test when they are ill. Test strips are available at drugstores. Ketones in the urine mean the diabetes is not under control. A doctor should be notified right away.

Diet

A healthy diet helps keep blood glucose in a normal range. It also can help people with type 2 diabetes lose weight.

The best diet for a person with diabetes is the best diet for anyone. It should contain food from each food group. Everyone should have grains, fruits, vegetables, meats, and dairy products every day. A healthy diet is low in fat. It is high in complex carbohydrates such as beans, vegetables, and grains. It contains a medium amount of protein.

People with diabetes have some special dietary rules. These people need the same amount of carbohydrates each day. They need to eat meals at the same time each day. They should not skip a meal. These rules make it easier to balance food and insulin.

At one time, doctors told people with diabetes to stay away from sweets. Doctors thought that sweets put too much glucose in the blood. New research gives a different picture. Simple carbohydrates (like sugar) and complex carbohydrates (like bread) raise glucose in the same way. People with diabetes can have small amounts of sweets. They then must eat less of something else. This helps them to stay within their carbohydrate count.

"There's one thing I really hate about my diabetes. I can't sleep late on Saturday morning. I have to get up, test my blood, and eat breakfast."
—Dan, age 14

Dietitians can help with meal planning. These diet specialists can suggest meal plans. The plans have the right number of calories for growth and consistent carbohydrate intake. Dietitians can show how to read labels for carbohydrates. Just about any food can be worked into the meal plan. Many cookbooks and recipes also are available for people with diabetes.

Stress

Stress can make glucose levels go up. It is important to learn how to manage stress. People with diabetes need to know what stresses them. Then they will know when to watch their glucose levels. They can take steps to avoid the stress.

Exercise

Exercise is another important part of controlling diabetes. Exercise uses up energy. Doing so helps lower blood sugar levels. It also reduces stress. Regular exercise and a healthy diet can help prevent type 2 diabetes. Regular exercise may require adding calories to the diet.

People with diabetes should see a doctor before beginning an exercise program. Most doctors encourage aerobic exercise for people with diabetes. Some types of aerobic exercise include walking, jogging, biking, and skating. These all strengthen the heart and lungs. They also are good for ensuring a safe weight. Teens with diabetes can play football, basketball, and other team sports. However, coaches need to know that an athlete has diabetes.

Exercise can lower glucose levels too much. People with diabetes may need to eat a snack before exercising. They should take along quick sugar such as hard candy or raisins. Testing blood sugar during exercise can be helpful. It can signal when levels are getting too low.

Tight Control or Standard Treatment

Matt and Nate each have type 1 diabetes. Matt **Matt, Age 16 & Nate, Age 17** gives himself insulin shots twice daily. He uses the same insulin dose each day. He also tests his blood sugar two times a day. Matt sees his doctor about four times a year.

Nate gives himself six or seven insulin shots each day. He tests his blood sugar throughout the day. Depending on the reading, he adjusts his insulin dose or food intake. Nate's health care team checks on him frequently.

Fast Fact

One study showed that people with type 1 who practiced tight control prevented or delayed long-term health problems. More than 1000 people in North America took part in the 10-year study. It ended in 1993.

There are two different ideas about diabetes treatment. Matt follows standard treatment. Most people with diabetes use this method. Nate follows tight control. This method tries to imitate the pancreas. It puts out a little insulin all the time. It gives extra insulin when food is eaten. Tight control is becoming more popular.

Doctors have different opinions about tight control. Studies show that it can reduce damage to kidneys and eyes by 50 to 60 percent. Many doctors start tight control for children during the elementary school or teen years. Another advantage of tight control is that it offers more freedom. People can eat more of the foods they want. They also can eat when they want.

Most doctors are using tight control for children with diabetes. However, others say it is too much work and too expensive. They worry that patients risk letting their blood glucose drop too low.

Points to Consider

What would be hard about following a treatment plan at school?

A teen with diabetes will be at your Halloween party. What food could you serve to fit his or her treatment plan?

How might a diabetic diet plan affect other family members?

How could you help a friend with diabetes stick to his or her treatment plan?

Would you choose standard treatment or tight control? Why?

Chapter Overview

Hypoglycemia means blood sugar is too low. Hyperglycemia means blood sugar is too high. Both conditions can be dangerous. People with diabetes should prepare for emergencies.

Uncontrolled diabetes can cause long-term health problems. Diabetes can damage the eyes, heart, kidneys, and nervous system. Most often the damage cannot be fixed.

People with diabetes are at even greater risk from the effects of smoking. Alcohol and other drugs also can be harmful.

Chapter 5

Emergencies and Long-Term Health Problems

Blood sugar levels that are out of control can cause problems. They can lead to medical emergencies such as hypoglycemia and hyperglycemia. These problems must be handled right away. Years of high blood sugar also can damage many parts of the body. Most often, there is no way to fix the damage.

Diabetes Emergency Kit

Teens with diabetes should carry an emergency kit for insulin reactions. Some items in the kit might be:

- Candy (5 to 6 hard candies)
- Raisins (2 tablespoons)
- Small tube of frosting or decorating gel
- Glucose tablets (3 to 4)
- Soda pop (not diet)
- Fruit juice (4 to 6 ounces)

Hypoglycemia

Gen grabbed a can of juice as she flew out the door. She had no time for breakfast this morning. She was already late. Gen was going to hang out with friends at the mall.

Gen, Age 16

By 11 o'clock, Gen was very hungry. She felt cold, shaky, and weak. Her head ached. Beads of sweat formed on her upper lip. "When are we going to stop for lunch?" she wondered to herself. Gen felt too embarrassed to say anything.

Kate saw that Gen was in trouble because Gen looked pale and confused. Kate knew that Gen needed some quick sugar. Kate reached in her backpack for a can of soda. She made Gen sit down and drink it. After a few minutes, Gen felt better. The girls headed for the food court.

Gen, who has type 1 diabetes, showed signs of hypoglycemia. *Hypo* means "under" or "below." Gen let her blood sugar drop too low (below 70 mg/dL). Not eating enough or waiting too long to eat can cause hypoglycemia. Too much insulin also can cause this condition. Hypoglycemia is sometimes called insulin reaction or insulin shock.

Hypoglycemia can be dangerous. It must be treated fast before the person possibly passes out. Luckily, Kate knew about Gen's diabetes. Gen had explained how to help in an emergency.

Hyperglycemia

Hyperglycemia is the opposite of hypoglycemia. *Hyper* means "above" or "beyond." The person's blood sugar becomes very high (above 240 mg/dL). Hyperglycemia happens to people who skip their insulin or take too little insulin. It also may happen during an illness.

Hyperglycemia develops over several days. Early symptoms include great thirst, excessive urination, and fatigue. Without insulin, ketones build up and poison the blood. Then the person experiences difficulty breathing, abdominal pain, and vomiting. Breath that smells like fruit is another sign. People with hyperglycemia need insulin to keep from going into a coma. They could die.

Friends and family can watch for signs of hyperglycemia. They can ask about the person's use of insulin. An unconscious person should not be given food or drink. It could go into the windpipe and cause choking. The person needs emergency treatment in a hospital.

Long-Term Health Problems

Diabetes can cause serious health problems. Research studies have shown that high blood sugar levels damage blood vessels. Every year thousands of people lose their eyesight because of diabetes. Diabetes is the leading cause of kidney failure. People with diabetes are two to four times more likely to have heart disease or a stroke.

High blood sugar also causes nerve damage. People with diabetes may lose feeling in their hands, feet, and legs. This happens because of reduced blood flow. Sometimes limbs must be amputated. This means that they must be surgically removed. Diabetes is the second-leading cause of lower limb amputations.

Poor blood flow can cause other problems in people with diabetes. These people may have sores that take a long time to heal. People with diabetes also are more likely to get gum disease. Gum disease can lead to tooth loss if untreated.

Diabetes is a costly health problem. In the United States, diabetes costs $92 billion each year. This includes money spent on treatment. It also includes money lost because people cannot work.

Controlling blood sugar is the best way to prevent long-term health problems. People with diabetes also can do the following:

Take care of health problems immediately

Have regular eye exams

Have regular urine checks

Have regular cholesterol checks

Treat sores and cuts immediately

Take extra care of legs and feet

Brush teeth after every meal, floss daily, and have a dental exam every six months

Smoking, Drinking, and Taking Drugs

There is another way to prevent long-term health problems. That involves not using tobacco, alcohol, or other drugs. Research has shown that smokers increase their risk of heart disease. Smokers who have diabetes increase their risk even more.

"Diabetes is a disease of choices. You can choose to control your disease or not."
—Derek, age 17

Alcohol has been linked to heart disease and nerve damage. It also adds calories to the diet. Alcohol lowers blood glucose and can lead to hypoglycemia. A person with hypoglycemia may seem drunk. Mike's story shows the dangers of mixing diabetes with drinking.

Mike is a high school senior with diabetes. **Mike, Age 18** He heard that some kids were having a keg party. He decided to drop by and check it out.

Mike had to pay $5 at the door. Someone put a plastic cup in his hand. Mike wasn't planning to drink. Then he thought, "A few beers won't kill me."

Mike didn't think about his empty stomach. After a few beers, he began to act strangely. He was having an insulin reaction. The others thought he was drunk and laughed at him. Mike staggered out of the house and passed out on the lawn. A man spotted him and rushed him to a hospital.

Alcohol and other drugs may cause people to forget to watch their blood sugar. Those people might forget to take their insulin. They may not care about eating a healthy diet and exercising.

Points to Consider

Who should know about a person's diabetes?

What choices does a person with diabetes have?

Should a person with diabetes be blamed for a diabetic emergency or a long-term health problem? Explain.

Chapter Overview

Living with diabetes can be hard for teens. They must deal with diabetes while juggling a busy schedule. Diabetes can interfere with having fun and dating. Physical changes during the teen years make diabetes hard to control.

Teens with diabetes must deal with feelings of anger and sadness. Talking to other teens with diabetes can help. Learning about the disease is another way to cope.

Teens with diabetes should seek the help of doctors and other health professionals. The love and support of family and friends can help, too.

Living with diabetes takes courage and hard work.

Chapter 6

Living With Diabetes

Living with diabetes can be difficult. It affects every area of a person's life. Diabetes can present special challenges to teenagers.

Teen Hormones

During the teen years, growth and sex hormones become active. These hormones make it harder to control blood sugar. Teens need to see a doctor who specializes in diabetes care. The doctor can adjust the treatment plan. It helps if the doctor is easy to talk with and a good listener.

"Diabetes is always with you. You can never take a vacation from it."
—Ellen, age 16

Juan is growing fast. His mother wondered **Juan, Age 15** about his self-testing. His numbers seemed to jump around too much. She thought Juan wasn't taking his insulin. The doctor explained to her about hormones. Juan's mother realized that he was doing fine.

Breaking Away

It is normal for teens to want more freedom. They want to separate themselves from their family. Teens with diabetes may have a harder time doing things on their own. Their parents may want to protect them. The parents may try to hold the teens back. These teens have to prove that they can be responsible with controlling their diabetes.

At the same time, teens might need help to manage their disease. There is a lot to remember. Teens who have the support of family members do much better. For example, the parents could buy supplies and make appointments. The teenager can take care of his or her own physical needs. This includes giving the shots, testing the blood, eating well, and exercising.

Fitting In

Teens with diabetes want to be like everyone else. They want to fit in. They may feel different because of the diabetes. They may rebel against their illness. This can be dangerous.

BernaDette didn't want anyone at school to know about her diabetes.
She was tired of the finger pricks and the insulin shots. She decided to forget about her treatment plan. Soon after, BernaDette passed out in the lunchroom. Now everyone in school knew about her disease. A counselor at the hospital talked with BernaDette. BernaDette saw that she had to face her disease and deal with it.

BernaDette, Age 14

Having Fun

Teens like to have fun. They may decide to go to a movie or stop for a burger and fries. Sometimes teens with diabetes cannot go along. They may need to stick to a schedule and a diet. They may not have their diabetes supplies with them. Other times, planning ahead allows teens with diabetes to join the fun. They can bring along the testing supplies. They also can calculate the carbohydrates according to their meal plan.

A person with diabetes cannot have the following jobs. The risk of an accident from an insulin reaction is too great.

- An airline pilot
- A soldier, sailor, or marine
- A construction worker on a tall building
- A school bus driver

Dating

Dating is important to teens. Teens with diabetes wonder if they should tell their dates about their illness. One girl tells her dates about her diabetes. Boys who accept this fact are the right ones for her. Another teen boy likes to meet girls on group dates. They find out about his diabetes that way. They may even see him having an insulin reaction. It is easier for him to ask girls out if they already know about him. Teens with diabetes need to do what makes them comfortable.

Getting a Job

Many teens get jobs after school or during the summer. Teens with diabetes may have problems getting a job.

> Joe applied for a job as a carryout person at a grocery store. He told the store manager about his diabetes. He said he might need breaks for snacks. He might need time out to test his blood sugar. Joe asked for a place to keep diabetes supplies. The store manager wasn't sure he wanted to hire Joe.
>
> Joe, Age 16

Joe and the store manager need to know about the Americans With Disabilities Act. This law protects the rights of people with diabetes. It says that employers must let employees take care of medical needs while on the job.

Feelings

Emotions go up and down during the teen years. Diabetes can add to a teen's emotional roller coaster. Teens may feel angry about their disease. They may feel sorry for themselves.

Teens can learn to deal with feelings of anger and sadness. One way is to talk about problems with people who understand. Some teens join support groups for teens with diabetes. Others log onto an Internet chat room for teens with diabetes.

Another way to deal with feelings is to learn more about diabetes. Hospitals and clinics have classes on diabetes. Many books and magazines are available. Teens who understand their disease feel more in control of it.

Most people feel better about themselves when they help others. Teens with diabetes could work at a camp for younger children with the disease. There teens can teach kids how to test their own blood and give themselves shots.

Coping With Diabetes

Teens who take charge of their diabetes improve their health. They feel good about themselves. If you are a teen with diabetes, you can do these things to cope with your illness:

Form a team of health care professionals.
Your team should include a medical doctor, a dietitian, a diabetes counselor, and an exercise instructor. You might find an endocrinologist, a doctor who specializes in diabetes. The team can help you come up with a treatment plan that's right for you.

Follow your treatment plan.
You not only will feel better now but also will help prevent health problems in the future. If there are problems with your treatment plan, discuss them with your health care team.

Get help for emotional problems.

It is normal to feel angry and sad from time to time. If these feelings do not go away, see a mental health counselor.

Form a support group of family and friends.

Take responsibility for self-care, but let your family help in some ways. It takes a lot of work to manage diabetes. You will do better with family support. Teach a few close friends about your diabetes. Tell them what to do in an emergency.

Learn all you can about diabetes.

You can learn about diabetes in classes, in magazines and books, and on the Internet. Join the American Diabetes Association or another diabetes organization. You will learn the latest information about diabetes.

Get to know other teens who have diabetes.

You can meet other teens with diabetes in support groups or in an Internet chat room. You might go to a camp for teens with diabetes. You can learn how others manage their illness. You also can share feelings and experiences. No one understands better than another teen with diabetes.

Teens should discuss their diabetes with school staff. They should find out the school policy on medications. Teens with diabetes have the right to:

- Eat a snack in the middle of class if necessary
- Go on class trips
- Make up work missed because of their illness

Tell your school about your diabetes.
Let your teachers and principal know your needs. Be sure they know how to handle a diabetic emergency. Find out school policy on bringing insulin to school. If you miss class because of your diabetes, see if you can make up the work. Always do your best and never use diabetes as an excuse to slack off.

Join the fight to make life better for people with diabetes.
Help to raise money for diabetes research if you like. Learn your rights as a person with diabetes. Become familiar with the Americans With Disabilities Act. Ask your legislators to pass other laws to help people with diabetes.

Help other people.

Teach younger kids with diabetes to deal with their illness. Visit elderly people who may be blind or disabled because of diabetes. Take the focus off yourself. You will see that other people have problems, too. You will feel better about yourself.

Points to Consider

What would you do if someone made fun of your diabetes?

What laws are needed to help people with diabetes?

What rights should a teen with diabetes have in school? What responsibilities?

Chapter Overview

Researchers are looking for better ways for people with diabetes to take insulin. Researchers also are looking for easier ways to check blood glucose.

Research is under way to prevent diabetes in at-risk people. This includes finding genes linked to diabetes.

Better ways of treating complications from diabetes are being developed.

A cure for diabetes may be in the future of today's teens.

Chapter 7

Looking Ahead

Dave was recently diagnosed with diabetes. "I'm not worried about my diabetes," he says. "By the time I'm 20, they'll have a cure."

Dave, Age 13

There may or may not be a cure for diabetes in the next few years. In the meantime, Dave should keep on with his treatment plan. He can count on one thing, though. Doctors and scientists are sure to find better ways to treat diabetes.

Myth: Eating lots of broccoli can cure diabetes.

Fact: Broccoli contains chromium. This mineral has been known to improve glucose tolerance. Diabetes is caused by a lack of insulin, not a lack of chromium. It is best to stick with balancing insulin, diet, and exercise. And broccoli is still healthful for other reasons.

Better Ways to Take Insulin

Many people with diabetes find it difficult to give themselves insulin shots. It is hard to know how much insulin to take. It is also hard to find the right time. Researchers are looking for better and easier ways for people with diabetes to take insulin.

A device that acts like a normal pancreas is one idea. Some people with type 1 diabetes already use an insulin pump. They wear this beeper-like device on a belt or in a pocket. It can be programmed to give insulin at certain times. Researchers are working on another kind of insulin pump. This pump would be put inside a person's body.

Transplant experiments are under way in Canada and in the United States. Researchers hope to put beta cells from a healthy pancreas into people with diabetes. A successful transplant would let the body produce insulin on its own. Operations to transplant an entire pancreas have had little success. The pancreas is more difficult to transplant than a heart or liver.

An insulin pill may soon be available. Researchers are close to inventing a special coating to surround the insulin. This coating would protect the insulin from stomach acids. There are other ideas for doing away with painful shots. These include spraying insulin up the nose or inhaling it by mouth with an inhaler.

Better Ways to Test Blood

Monitoring blood glucose several times a day is a lot of work. It is painful, too. Researchers are looking for painless ways to test blood. One idea has been called the dream beam. The person places a finger inside a monitor. A special light shines through the skin and measures blood glucose. Another idea is a skin patch. This patch would measure glucose levels through skin.

Still another idea is to put a monitoring device inside a person. This device would constantly measure blood glucose. An alarm would go off when levels are too high or too low.

Diabetes Prevention

Researchers are looking for ways to prevent diabetes. One area of research focuses on type 1 diabetes.

Anne's older sister, Sue, has type 1
diabetes. The girls' doctor tested Anne to see

if she is at risk for diabetes, too. The doctor used a test called
the islet-cell antibody test. This blood test looks for antibodies
that can destroy insulin-producing cells. These antibodies can
be in the blood many years before type 1 develops.

The test showed islet-cell antibodies in Anne's blood. The
doctor asked Anne to be part of a research study. She would
get low doses of insulin every day over the next five years. The
doctor explained the question that the researchers wanted to
answer: Can insulin prevent or delay type 1 diabetes in
at-risk people?

At first, Anne didn't like the idea of taking insulin. Then she
realized the study might keep her from getting diabetes. Anne
and her family agreed that she should be in the study.

Another area of research focuses on preventing type 2 diabetes.
Scientists have found genes linked to type 2. Genes carry traits
such as eye color and skin color. Some people have genes that
make it likely they will get diabetes. Scientists hope to replace
these faulty genes with normal genes.

The number of Americans with type 2 diabetes will increase in the coming years. The over-65 population is growing rapidly. Older Americans tend to be overweight. They also exercise little. This lifestyle puts them at risk for type 2 diabetes.

Preventing Long-Term Problems

Scientists are trying to find out why diabetes causes long-term health problems. They are looking for better methods of treatment. For example, researchers have found that laser treatments slow blindness in people with diabetes. New drugs show promise in preventing nerve and kidney damage.

Looking Ahead

Teens with diabetes can look forward to the future with hope. There may be a cure for diabetes in their lifetime. There will certainly be better ways of treating the disease. Teens who take charge of their diabetes improve their health. They feel good about themselves. Many people are working to make life better for those with diabetes.

Points to Consider

How can education play a role in preventing diabetes?

What school project could you do to help raise awareness of diabetes?

Would you take part in a study to prevent or cure a serious illness? Why or why not?

Glossary

amputation (am-pyoo-TAY-shuhn)—the removal of a body part by surgery

antibody (AN-ti-bah-dee)—a part of the body's defense system against germs

carbohydrate (kar-boh-HYE-drayt)—a food that the body breaks down into sugar or glucose

coma (KOH-muh)—a deep sleep caused by illness, injury, or poison

dietitian (dye-uh-TI-shuhn)—a person who helps people plan a diet for good health

glucose (GLOO-kohss)—a form of sugar the body needs for energy; the body makes glucose mainly from carbohydrates.

hormone (HOR-mohn)—a chemical produced by a gland or tissue; hormones enter the bloodstream and control various body processes.

hyperglycemia (hye-pur-glye-SEE-mee-uh)—very high blood sugar

hypoglycemia (hye-poh-glye-SEE-mee-uh)—very low blood sugar

immune system (i-MYOON SISS-tuhm)—the body system that fights disease

insulin (IN-suh-luhn)—a hormone that allows glucose to enter the body's cells; insulin is used to treat diabetes.

islets of Langerhans (EYE-luhtss OV LAHNG-uhr-hanz)—glands in the pancreas that produce insulin

ketone (KEE-tohn)—a poisonous acid produced when the body burns fat instead of sugar

pancreas (PAN-kree-uhss)—a small organ that produces insulin

urination (yur-uh-NAY-shuhn)—the act of passing urine from the body

For More Information

Betschart, Jean, and Susan Thom. *In Control: A Guide for Teens With Diabetes.* Minneapolis: Chronimed, 1995.

Ferber, Elizabeth. *Diabetes: One Day at a Time.* Brookfield, CT: Millbrook Press, 1996.

Huegel, Kelly. *Young People and Chronic Illness.* Minneapolis: Free Spirit, 1998.

Kelly, Pat. *Coping With Diabetes.* New York: Rosen, 1998.

Semple, Carol McCormick. *Health Watch: Diabetes.* Parsippany, NJ: Crestwood House, 1996.

Useful Addresses and Internet Sites

American Association of Diabetes Educators
100 West Monroe Street
Fourth Floor
Chicago, IL 60603-1901
1-800-338-3633

American Diabetes Association
1660 Duke Street
Alexandria, VA 22314
1-800-342-2383

Canadian Diabetes Association
15 Toronto Street, Suite 800
Toronto, ON M5C 2E3
CANADA
1-800-BANTING (in Canada)

Juvenile Diabetes Foundation International
120 Wall Street
New York, NY 10005-4001
1-800-JDF-CURE

Diabetes.com
http://www.diabetes.com
Informational site that helps people with
diabetes practice good self care

Diabetes Net
http://www.diabetesnet.com
Offers information on living well with diabetes

Children With Diabetes
http://www.childrenwithdiabetes.com
An on-line resource for kids with diabetes and
their families

Centers for Disease Control Diabetes and
Public Health Resource
http://www.cdc.gov/nccdphp/ddt/ddthome.htm
Translates scientific research on diabetes into
easily understandable language

Index

Index continued